Contents

First published in 1998

The Children's Society
Edward Rudolf House
Margery Street
London WC1X 0JL

A catalogue record of this book is available
from The British Library.

ISBN 1 899783 20 2

Foreword

This report is intended as a lesson and a warning. For the first time we have a picture of the information local education authorities collect about children who are permanently and temporarily excluded. It is an incomplete picture because some authorities have not managed to collate the information they need to begin to address this escalating problem. Even more worrying are the clearly inconsistent policies between authorities and even among schools within the same authority.

Children's futures hang on their schooling. Exclusions – both permanent and temporary – carry a heavy penalty. They disrupt a child's education: excluded children often receive only a part-time education and have no support when they return to mainstream school. This can lead to disillusion, and then to further disruptive behaviour. And for the children who drift onto the streets and towards crime, the route from primary school exclusion to prison can be frighteningly short.

The Government is to be commended for its initiatives on social exclusion and its proposal to impose financial penalties on schools who exclude children. Our survey revealed LEAs whose practice could serve as a blueprint for others to follow. But even with these developments, the overall impression from this survey is that lack of information on the one hand and lack of understanding on the other, continue to ensure that far more children are excluded for far longer than necessary. The current paucity of information collected by some LEAs and schools is inexcusable. The result of this failure is that children are having their education undermined and their futures blighted.

The Children's Society runs two innovative projects in schools that work with teachers, pupils and parents, to help solve the problems of disruptive children. The report lists recommendations that we believe would improve education for children at risk of exclusion, and benefit their teachers, their parents, and the pupils who share their classes. We know that our projects have made a difference to children's lives and we want to see others reap the benefit of that experience.

When we talk about investing in the future, about hope for the new millennium, about encouraging children to have a stake in the future, we must start from a position of strength and faith. We need to believe that we can work with children and support them through their difficulties.

IAN SPARKS
Chief Executive
The Children's Society

Introduction

School exclusion: A growing problem

Exclusion means being shut out. (School student, Merthyr Tydfil)

Exclusion is removing the problem and not solving it. (Pupil referral unit student, Kent).

Exclusion amounts to state-sanctioned truancy. (Ian Sparks, Chief Executive, The Children's Society)

School exclusions are rising at an alarming rate. In the last five years the number has increased by 300 per cent. In the academic year 1995/6 the Department for Education and Employment (DfEE) recorded 12,476 permanent exclusions. Figures collected by independent research (Parsons, 1996a) record a higher figure of 13,581, representing a rise of 450 per cent over the last five years.

In addition, there is a much larger number of temporary or 'fixed-term' exclusions, perhaps as many as 135,000 in the year 1995/6, although records of these are sometimes incomplete.

There is a further hidden figure of children who are informally excluded, where children are told to leave school or parents are asked to withdraw them for brief periods, as a form of punishment or for a 'cooling off' period.

Excluded children often get very limited educational support, while parents are left to cope with work and childcare arrangements at very short notice. When children return, few schools have programmes to deal with them. As a result, some of them fall further behind, and become disillusioned and disruptive in class.

A number of trends are of particular concern. First, the number of exclusions is rising most rapidly in primary schools. When children as young as four are being excluded, it is clear that there is a crisis in our education system.

Another trend which is extremely worrying is the number of African Caribbean boys who are excluded.

Other groups, too, are disproportionately represented. Young people in care are estimated to make up 33 per cent of all secondary school exclusions and 66 per cent of all primary school exclusions (DfEE, unpublished).

These destructive patterns benefit no-one. They mean that children are relegated to the margins of society while teachers find it difficult to cope, and the public picks up the cost for children who drift onto the streets without qualifications and skills where they can easily gravitate towards crime and prison.

Forty-two per cent of school age offenders have been excluded by the time they appear in court. In a recent Children's Society study of persistent young offenders (Crowley, 1998), only one of the sample of 19 was in full-time schooling. Most of the others had been excluded and as a result their schooling had broken down.

Excluded students remain entitled to receive an education, but this is often only part-time, and does not cover the full curriculum. In addition, there is a risk of 'reinforcement' of problem behaviour if the current practice continues of providing increasing numbers of pupil referral units (PRUs), and thereby increasing the capacity for 'the education... of children otherwise than at school'.

It would have helped me if I'd stayed at school. If I weren't naughty it would have helped me you know. (PRU student, Kent)

The policy context

In the context of mounting concern about school exclusions, a number of policy initiatives have emerged. As far back as 1989, the Elton Committee report, *Discipline in Schools*, included a substantial number of recommendations relating to the management of problematic behaviour in schools. As a consequence, the 1993 Education Act changed the policy framework covering exclusions, withdrawing the option of indefinite exclusions, and leaving schools with a choice between 'fixed-term' (up to 15 days in any school term) or 'permanent' exclusions (which must be based on clear and rigorous procedures to protect the interests of all those affected). These legislative changes were supported by a series of Department for Education (DFE) circulars issued in 1994, relating to the management of discipline and welfare in schools and specifically the administration of exclusions.

Circular 10/94 outlined the responsibilities of schools and education authorities in relation to exclusion, and remains in force, subject to revision by the 1997 Education Act, which changed the maximum period of fixed-term exclusions to 45 days in any school year. The circular expresses a central underlying principle:

Unless other suitable arrangements are made, all children should be in school and learning. Exclusion should be used sparingly in response to serious breaches of school policy or law.

The circular strongly discourages unnecessary use of powers to exclude, stressing that permanent exclusions should only be used as a last resort. It also sets out a range of options available for use before exclusion, emphasising that some schools appear better able to avoid excluding pupils than others.

The circular also discourages other practices which appear to evade legal requirements, such as encouraging parents to withdraw their children from school 'voluntarily', thereby avoiding the stigma of exclusion, but in the process bypassing formal procedures which offer pupils and their parents important safeguards.

For students subject to exclusion, the 1993 Education Act, supported by DFE circular 11/94, clarifies the legal status of pupil referral units. Such units are now fairly widespread, and aim to provide an effective education for pupils who are 'out of school', whether because of exclusion or for other reasons.

In addition to these recent legislative developments and practical guidance, schools are now required to file annual returns of permanent exclusion figures to the DfEE. Local education authorities (LEAs) also collect information on all types of exclusion. However, as The Children's Society's survey demonstrates, they are often unable to gather comprehensive information, partly because of a number of flaws in current policy. Grant-maintained schools are not required to inform LEAs of fixed-term exclusions; and LEA schools do not always notify their authorities of exclusions of less than five days, as they are not obliged to do so. The latter is particularly unfortunate as it removes the opportunity to build up a picture of the relationship between early short-term exclusions, and subsequent longer or permanent exclusions – which might be of considerable value in enabling us to understand the trajectory of students' exclusion 'careers'.

Currently, the Government is consulting widely on further initiatives to tackle exclusions. The development of Education Action Zones, the recent guidance on behaviour policies and the commitment of the Social Exclusion Unit all underline the fact that significant opportunities to make positive progress are now available. In addition, a range of public and voluntary agencies are beginning to turn their attention to the task of first understanding and then finding effective alternatives to school exclusions. This impetus has been supported by a number of key research initiatives.

Despite these wide-ranging developments, the picture remains fragmented and unclear, and so far there has been little systematic development of strategies to tackle or prevent exclusions.

The evidence so far

The Office for Standards in Education (OFSTED) report, *Exclusions from Secondary Schools 1995/6*, documents a worrying level of inconsistency in practice and procedures. The report observes considerable variation in both LEA and school exclusion rates which, it states, cannot simply be attributed to differing school populations.

The report also underlines concerns about the disproportionate exclusion of black pupils, and the relatively poor levels of monitoring which contribute to the masking of such trends.

On the positive side, OFSTED notes that good school behaviour policies can contribute to reducing exclusion levels.

The Commission for Racial Equality (CRE) has estimated that up to 14,000 pupils are permanently excluded each year, and that black boys and girls are between four and six times more likely to be excluded than their white peers. The CRE also criticises the quality of recording practices among schools and questions the absence of processes by which formal commitments to equality of opportunity are put into practice. The CRE report estimates that the cost of providing alternative education for an excluded pupil is £4300 per year, twice that of a place in mainstream school.

Figures issued by the DfEE in October 1997 tell a similar story (see Tables in Appendix 2). For example, the great majority of primary schools report no permanent exclusions in the school year 1995/6, an achievement matched by about a quarter of all secondary schools; on the other hand, 1 in 5 secondary schools report more than five permanent exclusions in that period.

The DfEE figures also demonstrate that African-Caribbean pupils are excluded at a rate almost five times that which could be expected from their number in the general school population. Boys outnumber girls by about 5 to 1 with respect to permanent exclusions.

Their figures also illustrate a significant diversity between local education authorities, with variations in secondary school exclusions between 0.54 per cent (Doncaster) and 0.19 per cent (Kirklees) in the Yorkshire region alone, for example. The national norm is 0.34 per cent.

Given this wide-ranging evidence of a severe and worrying problem, The Children's Society is currently seeking to develop a better understanding of the nature of practice relating to exclusions, and the extent of variations between schools and different local authority areas. The aim is to draw on this understanding to develop a coherent programme to improve the chances of young people at risk of exclusion, and to ensure that there is an effective behaviour and education strategy in place to enable them to attain their full potential.

Survey results

Yes, I've got a right to an education, man, but I just fluffed it up before I had a chance to sort it out. (PRU student, Kent)

In January and February 1998, The Children's Society carried out a survey of local education authorities' current practices in relation to school exclusions. The survey questionnaire (see Appendix 1) was sent to 104 local education authorities and 66 responded, representing just under half of all the LEAs in England and Wales. Most provided full information about their record on exclusions, their recording methods, and their policies relating to excluded pupils. Two subsequently wrote to say they were unable to assist with the survey.

The figures relate to the 1996/7 academic year. Some authorities referred to work in progress, or work being developed. Clearly many authorities are already sensitive to the growing problem of exclusions and are working to develop effective solutions.

Types of exclusion

There are two types of exclusion, reflecting the seriousness with which the school views a pupil's behaviour.

Permanent exclusions used to be known as expulsions. When a child is excluded, he or she is removed from the school roll and the school is no longer *in loco parentis* for the pupil and has no further responsibility for that child. Schools are required by law to inform LEAs whenever a child has been permanently excluded.

Fixed-term exclusions – which used to be known as suspensions – are informal and usually last between one and five days. These are used as a form of punishment for bad behaviour and there is no legal require-ment to inform the local education authority. However, as a matter of good practice, it is essential to keep records so that children's behaviour and progress can be monitored.

Permanent exclusions

For the 64 respondents who completed the form, there were 838 primary and 5085 secondary permanent exclusions during 1996/7, making a total of 5923 permanent exclusions. These ranged from peak figures of 303 secondary and 66 primary exclusions in one area to two secondary and no primary cases in another authority. In general, this variation reflected the differing sizes and pupil numbers of the authorities con-cerned, although it was not the largest which recorded the highest number of exclusions.

Permanent secondary exclusions outnumbered those in primary schools by around 6 to 1, but this should not reduce the sense of concern about the situation in the primary sector. Permanently excluding children under the age of 11 can significantly damage their prospects at a very early age.

Temporary exclusions

The responses from local authorities on temporary exclusions were mixed. This partly reflects the fact that schools are not legally required to report exclusions of less than five days to the local education authority. Some concern about the reliability of information from non-LEA schools was also evident from the survey.

A second reason for the mixed response was the quality of record-keeping in some local education authorities.

The authorities fell into two categories:

• Eleven authorities could not provide even an estimate of temporary exclusions and some thought it quite unrealistic to do so.

• The other authorities (53) offered figures, although some observed that they were not entirely confident about their accuracy.

For the responding authorities, the overall figure for fixed-term exclusions was 49,730. This figure relates to the number of exclusions rather than numbers of *pupils* affected. This is an important distinction as some children will be excluded more than once, and it is these pupils who are more likely to end up permanently excluded.

This figure includes wide variations between authorities with one of the larger authorities recording 5424 temporary exclusions during 1996/7.

Four small authorities recorded less than 100 fixed-term exclusions and several authorities, including one major city, recorded fewer than 250.

Some authorities were able to provide numbers of individual pupils temporarily excluded. Using these figures, it is possible to estimate that around 30,000 individual pupils were temporarily excluded from school in the 64 responding authorities.

Assuming that the ratio of fixed-term to permanent exclusions recorded by the 53 authorities giving figures is the same on the national scale, the number of temporary exclusions recorded can be used to estimate a national figure. In these authorities, the ratio of fixed-term exclusions to permanent exclusions is 11 to 1. The DfEE national figure for permanent exclusions in 1995/6 was 12,476 (see Table 1, p. 15), suggesting *an estimated figure of over 135,000 fixed-term exclusions in England and Wales during the year 1995/6.*

Authorities were also asked to specify the average length of fixed-term exclusions, to try to establish whether or not there is any consistency of approach.

Forty per cent of those responding said that their records did not enable them to provide a figure, mainly because they believed they were not in possession of full information from schools. Interestingly, amongst those who did provide a figure there was comparatively little variation, with most reporting a norm of 3–5 days. The median was 3.5, and the mean average 4 days. Very few areas varied widely from this figure.

Excluded children – who are they?

The survey also asked for a breakdown of the gender and ethnic background of excluded children.

Ethnic background

Only just over half the responding authorities (58%) keep records of the ethnic background of those who are excluded. Where ethnic monitoring is carried out, the approach taken, the categories used and the level of detail achieved vary enormously.

Despite this, the survey supports evidence that a disproportionate number of black boys are excluded. In one local authority area, white pupils are a minority of those excluded.

Two serious concerns arise from these findings; firstly, they confirm that black school children are over-represented in school exclusion figures. Secondly, they show that ethnic monitoring in relation to school exclusions lacks any kind of coherence or national framework.

Gender

Rather more authorities were able to provide a gender breakdown and there was a surprising degree of consistency in the information gathered. Of the 59 local authorities who answered this question, 39 provided a gender breakdown.

The ratio of boys to girls was almost always in the range of between 4 and 5 to 1.

This suggests that there is indeed a substantial over-representation of boys excluded, but also that girls form a significant minority (16–20 per cent), so gender appropriate services must be developed.

Children in care

Fewer than half those who answered the question (38%) had any idea how many of those excluded were in local authority care. This is surprising in a context where social exclusion is becoming a priority issue and links between being in care, exclusion and other problems such as poverty, family disruption and crime are becoming more clearly identified.

Several authorities have thorough and detailed records of children's links with social workers and the care systems. A number of others (13) were able to give fairly precise figures of those known to be looked after by social services, whilst a similar number appeared to have a rough idea of this figure, and supplied an estimate.

Perhaps unsurprisingly, these figures in turn varied quite widely, with 12 authorities reporting less than 5 per cent of excluded pupils as being cared for by social services, five putting the figure between 5 and 10 per cent, and a further five specifying 10 per cent or more. One authority suggested that as many as 30% of its excluded students were in care.

Other figures have indicated that up to one third of those excluded are in care, but our survey does not give us a great deal of confidence in the accuracy of this estimate, since so many authorities simply have no idea of the figure.

Clearly, better knowledge and understanding of the links between exclusion and young people's experience of care are urgently needed.

Reasons for exclusion

Although the information was not requested, it was evident from those authorities that provided more detailed information that there is little consistency in recording reasons for exclusion.

According to pupils' own perceptions, reasons can be many and varied:

I kept on swearing, I was always getting angry and that's it. (PRU student, south London)

I was quite lippy at school. I refused to work and stuff. (PRU student, Kent)

Sometimes it's one thing that got you excluded at the end, but there were all sorts of things happening before. (PRU student, Kent)

They said 'yes, you are on contract' and I had to sign a bit of paper. They wrote down the rules they wanted you to follow so as they say, be on time for school, don't bunk no more.... On the contract, if you break one rule on the contract bit of paper, then you are out. (PRU student, Kent)

Sometimes, too, students question the fairness of these decisions:

Other people got worse than me and they are still there [in mainstream school]. (PRU student, Kent)

Clearly, detailed information about reasons for exclusion is essential in developing effective strategies and identifying possible discrimination in relation to particular groups. It is debatable, however, whether recording reasons for exclusion under sweeping categories such as 'disruption', without further explanation, will contribute much to our understanding about how and why key decisions, such as whether or not to exclude, are taken in school. Accurate and specific information needs to be pin-pointed to discover the precise causes for exclusions.

Inconsistencies

Our survey found enormous variations not just between authorities, but also within local authority areas and between schools in rates of exclusion. Most of the authorities surveyed were able to quote both primary and secondary schools that made no use of their powers to exclude during the academic year 1996/7. On the other hand, they also identified schools which made very substantial use of these powers.

The highest figures recorded for any one secondary school for fixed-term exclusions was 469 in the year, that is over two exclusions per school day.

In the same local authority, one primary school excluded pupils on 48 occasions, more than one in every school week.

These wide variations raise enormous questions about school ethos, coherent policies, social context, recording practices and issues of fairness and equity. This indicates a pressing need to establish a consistent framework and strategy for exclusions. This applies in particular to the processes by which fixed-term exclusions are imposed, given that they are less likely to be subject to formal frameworks and criteria. Despite the attempts of the Department for Education to instil consistency by means of circular 10/94 issued following the 1993 Education Act, schools are still apparently not behaving in a similar fashion. Much effort needs to be put into developing a common approach.

Behaviour policies

Our final question sought to identify whether or not authorities had behaviour policies in place to deal with the problems associated with exclusion. Several authorities were 'working on' their policies, clearly conscious that under the 1997 Education Act that they will need to have them in place by September 1998.

Despite this, more than half of those answering this question did not have a policy in place at the time of the survey. Of those who did, only a few had anything which could be said to be comprehensive.

However, several of these were high quality documents which provide an effective basis for tackling exclusion. It was probably no coincidence that those few were authorities recording a decline in the number of exclusions since the previous academic year. This is an encouraging finding, because it indicates that an active approach to controlling and tackling the problem of school exclusions can pay dividends. Clearly, there may be value in ensuring that such good practice is more widely disseminated.

What can be done about exclusions?

Much of the preceding evidence is disturbing, and documents a rapidly worsening situation in relation to school exclusion. The Children's Society is developing a programme of work to help schools deal with problem behaviour.

The Children's Society practice

Schools Have Inclusive Education (SHINE)

The Children's Society's SHINE Project works in two primary schools in south London. It has been in operation since September 1996, with workers in the schools since December 1996. There are two part-time workers and one full-time project manager.

The project's long-term goals are to reduce exclusion and to create an inclusive school environment and practice, particularly relying on improved communication between teachers, parents and children. The project operates from a whole school perspective which seeks to integrate all children, regardless of their difficulties, in a mainstream school.

Recognising that there are many personal and social factors associated with disruptive pupils, the project offers individual programmes of support, including one-to-one sessions, work with small groups and an in-class service for pupils referred as excluded or at risk of being excluded. Workers also carry out home visits and there is a drop-in for parents each week. Team members function as a channel of communication between parents, teachers and children.

The project also works across the school with the pupils in class groups. The workers have been successful in using a variety of methods for engaging the children in discussion about school issues. The children have enthusiastically taken up the theme of inclusion/exclusion and want to address this issue in the first instance by tackling issues such as bullying.

In-service training is being developed which will focus on positive approaches to difficult behaviour. It will be available for teachers, and also classroom and playground assistants. This is in recognition that playtime and lunchtime are the most likely times for fights and other incidents which lead to exclusion.

An evaluation at the end of the first year of operation (December 1997) indicated that there had been a reduction in the use of exclusions in the schools in which the project is operating. Changes in school policy and practice to promote inclusion also took place.

The Genesis Project

The Genesis Project works in a comprehensive school in south-east London. The Children's Society was approached by the school which identified specific needs within the school, such as behaviour problems and poor relationships both between staff and students and between students. The aim of the project is to develop strategies to assist with the inclusion of children and young people, to work preventatively and supportively within the school. A key element of this approach is increasing the participation of children and young people in the education system.

The project began in September 1995 and operates within the school. It has a project manager, a senior practitioner, a part-time outreach worker, an administrator/information worker, and uses sessional workers for one-to-one work. There is also a volunteer programme and a volunteer coordinator.

Students come to the project as self-referrals, and through referral from teachers (for a variety of issues, frequently triggered by behavioural problems in class, truancy and exclusion issues). The project also works with parents, carers and teachers.

The project services include providing information, advice, support, counselling, mediation and training to children and young people, teachers, parents and carers.

Key workers use a combination of one-to-one counselling with a structured programme designed and agreed between the student, the school and the Genesis Project. The project also makes referrals to other agencies including child guidance, social services, the specialist education department and other projects as appropriate.

The project has initiated and developed a student advisory group that discusses the views, opinions and concerns of representatives from each year. The project facilitates the group with the aim of identifying ways for the young people to become more involved in the fabric of school life, and to experience a sense of responsibility.

Students with behaviour problems and those at risk of both fixed-term and permanent exclusion or already excluded are given support, counselling and mediation. Project workers also attend governors' meetings and try to ensure that parents and students know their rights and understand their responsibilities in the school context. This meeting can also be used as an intervention strategy for young people at risk of exclusion, with the involvement of parents.

Conclusion and recommendations

The evidence from this survey suggests some worrying trends. Firstly, there are a very substantial number of exclusions, both permanent and fixed-term, from schools right across the country. In addition, there is real evidence of a substantial problem amongst primary school children which would not even have been contemplated ten years ago.

Schools and local authorities appear to vary widely in their records relating to exclusions, but no clear reason for this emerged from the survey. Other studies have indicated that school ethos, school behaviour policies, and consistent discipline affect the need to resort to exclusions. The wide variations in the survey suggest an urgent need for better training and wide dissemination of such examples of good practice as are available.

Our survey confirmed earlier concerns about the disproportionate number of black students and students living in care who are excluded. But we are also greatly concerned that many local education authorities appeared unable to operate an effective ethnic monitoring system.

Clearly a need for better information systems and improved communication between schools and local education authorities is indicated. Indeed, there is public concern about the inadequacy of the data on which local policies and strategies need to be based. There is a role for government to establish a national framework for the collection and interpretation of exclusions data.

The overall impression, then, is one of a severe and growing problem, for which a limited range of solutions is available, and where the information necessary to form an accurate picture is incomplete.

The Children's Society therefore makes the following recommendations to move matters towards a solution:

(i) **The Government should draw up a comprehensive national framework for the collation and interpretation of data on both fixed-term and permanent exclusions.**

(ii) **Pupils excluded from school for whatever reason should receive a full-time alternative education.**

(iii) **Exclusions should be regularly reviewed, with a presumption in favour of pupils being readmitted. In other words, it must be demonstrated that there is a continuing need to exclude that particular individual.**

(iv) **Exclusions should not take place without a mandatory case conference, involving the child, parent, school, edu-**

cation authority and other relevant people, to take place within seven days of the decision. The case conference should include a re-integration plan for the pupil.

(v) Excluded pupils are currently removed from the school roll. This arrangement means the school has no responsibility to re-integrate excluded pupils.
Children excluded from school should remain on the school roll, even if they are being educated elsewhere.

(vi) Performance indicators, such as league tables, effectively encourage schools to exclude difficult children rather than retain them. Children who have behaviour problems incur additional costs for schools.
Schools should no longer face disincentives to retain children at risk of exclusion. Additional payment for children with special needs must be provided when required.

(vii) **Procedures for exclusion should be fully documented, and provide clear and explicit information for parents and children. Appropriate safeguards and appeals procedures should be made available.**

(viii) **Effective information, advice and counselling services should be available to parents with children at risk of or experiencing exclusion.**

(ix) Teachers appear to have little training in behaviour management and understandably struggle when faced with persistent disruptive behaviour.
Teacher training must be extended to develop inter-personal and problem-solving skills, and to support teachers trying to develop a better understanding of how to deal with difficult and challenging behaviour.

(x) **A good practice consultancy should be established as a national resource for schools and local authorities to improve their own ability to prevent exclusions.**

(xi) **Imaginative schemes to help tackle exclusions should be encouraged and funded accordingly.**

(xii) **The voluntary sector should be considered a legitimate partner in schemes to tackle exclusions.**

Appendix 1: Survey questionnaire

Thank you for agreeing to take part in this research. Please fill in the answers to the questions in the spaces provided.

1. How many students were permanently excluded from primary and secondary schools in the academic year 1996/7?

    Primary ....

    Secondary ....

2. Do you keep a record of temporary exclusions? (*please circle*)   **YES   NO**

    If you do, how many temporary exclusions
    were there in the school year 1996/7?   ....

    If you do not, please give an estimate   ....

    How many students does this represent?   ....

3. Do you keep a record of the ethnic backgrounds
    and genders of excluded students? (*please circle*)   **YES   NO**

If you do keep such records, please provide a copy on a separate sheet

3.1 If you do not, when do you expect to have this in place? ....

4. What proportion of excluded students are in care?   ....%

5. How much variation was there in exclusion rates between schools in the 1996/7 academic year?

    What is the highest figure in primary schools? ....

    What is the lowest figure in primary schools? ....

    What is the highest figure in secondary schools? ....

    What is the lowest figure in secondary schools? ....

6. What is the average length of time that temporarily excluded students are out of school? .... **days** .... **weeks** .... **months?**

7. Do you have a behaviour support policy
    to respond to exclusions? (*please circle*)   **YES   NO**

    If you do, please provide a copy on a separate sheet.

    Please include the following details for our own (confidential) records:

    Name ....

    Job Title ....

    Education Authority ....

    Tel. number ....

Thank you for completing this questionnaire. If you have any additional comments, please feel free to include them with your fax.

Appendix 2: Tables

Table 1 Number of permanent exclusions by type of school (England 1994/5 and 1995/6)

	1994/5		
	Number of permanent exclusions (1)	Percentage of permanent exclusions (2)	Percentage of school population (3)
Primary	1,365	12	0.03
Secondary (4)	9,197	83	0.31
Special (5)	522	5	0.53
All schools	11,084	100	0.15

	1995/6		
	Number of permanent exclusions (1)	Percentage of permanent exclusions (2)	Percentage of school population (3)
Primary	1,608	13	0.04
Secondary (4)	10,344	83	0.34
Special (5)	524	4	0.54
All schools	12,476	100	0.19

Source: Department for Education and Employment (press release, 1997)

(1) The number of permanent exclusions was estimated to take account of a small number of schools that did not provide any information on their permanent exclusions

(2) The number of permanent exclusions expressed as a percentage of the total number of permanent exclusions

(3) The number of permanent exclusions expressed as a percentage of the number (headcount) of full- and part-time pupils of all ages (excluding dually registered pupils in special schools) in January each year

(4) Includes middle schools as deemed secondary

(5) Includes both maintained and non-maintained special schools

Table 2 Distribution of the number of permanent exclusions over schools by type of school (England 1995/6)

Number of exclusions per school	Number of schools		
	Primary	Secondary	Special
0	17,108	974	942
1–2	1,331	1,150	272
3–4	36	627	41
5–6	5	381	6
7–8	0	216	1
9–10	0	114	1
11–15	0	100	0
16–20	0	29	0
21+	0	3	0

Source: Department for Education and Employment (press release, 1997)

Table 3 Number of permanent exclusions by gender (England 1995/6)

	Number of permanent exclusions	Percentage of permanent exclusions (1)	Percentage of school population (2)
All pupils (3)	12,476	100	0.19
Boys	10,365	83	0.27
Girls	2,111	17	0.06

Source: Department for Education and Employment (press release, 1997)

(1) The number of permanent exclusions expressed as a percentage of the total number of permanent exclusions

(2) The number of permanent exclusions expressed as a percentage of the number (headcount) of full- and part-time pupils of all ages in primary, secondary and special schools (excluding dually registered pupils in special schools) in January 1996

(3) Includes maintained primary, secondary and special and non-maintained special schools

Table 4 Number of permanent exclusions of pupils of compulsory school age by ethnic group (England 1995/6)

| Of whom: | Number of pupils (1) | Percentage of pupils (2) | Permanent exclusions | | |
			Number of permanent exclusions (3)	Percentage of permanent exclusions (4)	Percentage of school population (5)
White	5,634,453	88.9	10,096	82.6	0.18
Black Caribbean	94,308	1.5	867	7.1	0.92
Black African	61,288	1.0	216	1.6	0.35
Black Other	45,171	0.7	241	2.0	0.53
Indian	157,911	2.5	109	0.9	0.07
Pakistani	155,350	2.5	255	2.1	0.16
Bangladeshi	59,570	0.9	58	0.5	0.10
Chinese	22,727	0.4	14	0.1	0.05
Any other ethnic group	107,850	1.7	366	3.0	0.34
Totals	6,338,628	100.0	12,232	100.0	0.19

Source: Department for Education and Employment (press release, 1997)

(1) The number (headcount) of full- and part-time pupils of compulsory school age in primary, secondary and special schools, excluding dually registered pupils in special schools, in January 1996, distributed over ethnic groups in accordance with the distribution of pupils of compulsory school age and above in primary and secondary schools over ethnic groups in January 1997

(2) The number (headcount) of full- and part-time pupils of compulsory school age and above in primary and secondary schools expressed as a percentage of the total number of pupils of compulsory school age and above in these schools in January 1997

(3) Includes 10 permanent exclusions of pupils unclassified according to ethnic group

(4) The number of permanent exclusions of compulsory school age expressed as a percentage of the total number of permanent exclusions of compulsory school age

(5) The number of permanent exclusions of compulsory school age expressed as a percentage of the number (headcount) of full- and part-time pupils of compulsory school age in primary, secondary and special schools (excluding dually registered pupils in special schools) in January 1996

References and further reading

Advisory Centre for Education (1993) *Children out of School: A Guide for Parents and Schools on Non-attendance at School*. London: ACE.

Brodie, I. and Berridge, D. (1996) *School Exclusion: Research Themes and Issues*. Luton: University of Luton Press.   *7 . 50*

Cohen, R., Hughes, M. and Ashworth, L. *et al.* (1994) *School's Out: The Family Perspective on School Exclusion*. London: Family Service Units.

Commission for Racial Equality (1996) *Exclusion from School: The Public Cost*. London: CRE.

Commission for Racial Equality (1997) *Exclusions from School and Racial Equality: A Good Practice Guide*. London: CRE.

Committee of Enquiry into Discipline in Schools (1989) *Discipline in Schools: Report of the Committee of Enquiry chaired by Lord Elton*. London: HMSO.

Crowley, A. (1998) *A Criminal Waste: A Study of Child Offenders Eligible for Secure Training Centres*. London: The Children's Society.

Department for Education (1994) *Exclusions from School: Circular number 10/94*. London: Department for Education.

Hayden, C. (1997) *Children Excluded from Primary School: Debates, Evidence, Responses*. Buckingham: Open University Press.

Hayden, C. (1996) *Primary Age Children Excluded from School: Report no 33*. Portsmouth: Social Services Research and Information Unit.

Hyams-Parish, A. (1996) *Banished to the Exclusion Zone: School Exclusions and the Law from the Viewpoint of the Child*. Colchester: Children's Legal Centre.

Jordan, L. and Goodey, C. (1996) *Human Rights and School Change: The Newham Story*. Bristol: Centre for Studies on Inclusive Education.

Kent County Council (1996) *Affective Schools Action Project*. Maidstone: Kent County Council Education Department.

Martin, C. and Hayman, S. (1997) *Absent from School: Truancy and Exclusion*. London: Institute for the Study and Treatment of Delinquency.

OFSTED (1996) *Exclusions from Secondary Schools 1995/6*. London: The Stationery Office.

Osler, A. (1997) *Exclusion from School and Racial Equality: Research Report*. London: Commission for Racial Equality.

Parsons, C. (1994) *Excluding Primary School Children*. London: Family Policy Studies Centre.

Parsons, C. (1996a) 'Permanent exclusions from schools in England: Trends, causes and responses.' *Children and Society*, vol. 10, pp. 177 186.

Parsons, C. (1996b) *Measuring the Real Cost of Excluding Children from School*. London: National Children's Bureau.

Reid, H. (1997) *School and Social Work: Truancy, Exclusion, and Special Education*. Norwich: Social Work Monographs No 156.

Runnymede Trust (1996) *This is where I live: Stories and Pressures in Brixton*. London: Runnymede Trust.

The Children's Society

A positive force for change

The Children's Society is one of Britain's leading charities for children and young people. Founded in 1881 as a Christian organisation, The Children's Society reaches out unconditionally to children and young people regardless of race, culture or creed.

Over 90 projects throughout England and Wales

We work with over 30,000 children of all ages, focusing on those whose circumstances have made them particularly vulnerable. We aim to help stop the spiral into isolation, anger and lost hope faced by so many young people.

We constantly look for effective, new ways of making a real difference

We measure local impact and demonstrate through successful practice that major issues can be tackled and resolved. The Children's Society has an established track record of taking effective action: both in changing public perceptions about difficult issues such as child prostitution, and in influencing national policy and practice to give young people a better chance at life.

The Children's Society is committed to overcoming injustice wherever we find it

We are currently working towards national solutions to social isolation, lack of education and the long-term problems they cause, through focused work in several areas:

• helping parents whose babies have stopped eating, endangering their development;
• involving children in the regeneration of poorer communities;
• preventing exclusions from primary and secondary schools;
• providing a safety net for young people who run away from home and care;
• seeking viable alternatives to the damaging effects of prison for young offenders.

The Children's Society will continue to raise public awareness of difficult issues to promote a fairer society for the most vulnerable children in England and Wales. For further information about the work of The Children's Society or to obtain a publications catalogue, please contact:

> The Publishing Department,
> The Children's Society,
> Edward Rudolf House,
> Margery Street,
> London WC1X 0JL.
> Tel. 0171 837 4299. Fax 0171 837 0211.

The Children's Society is a registered charity: Charity Registration No. 221124.